Washington, D.C.

By Simone T. Ribke

Consultant
Nanci R. Vargus, Ed.D.
Assistant Professor of Literacy
University of Indianapolis, Indianapolis, Indiana

Children's Press®
A Division of Scholastic Inc.
New York   Toronto   London   Auckland   Sydney
Mexico City   New Delhi   Hong Kong
Danbury, Connecticut

Designer: Herman Adler Design
Photo Researcher: Caroline Anderson
The photo on the cover shows the Capitol building.

Library of Congress Cataloging-in-Publication Data

Ribke, Simone T.
  Washington, D.C. / by Simone T. Ribke.
      p. cm. – (Rookie read-about geography)
Includes index.
Summary: A brief introduction to the geography and people of Washington, D.C.
  ISBN 0-516-22744-0 (lib. bdg.)   0-516-27897-5 (pbk.)
  1. Washington (D.C.)–Juvenile literature. 2. Washington (D.C.)–Geography–Juvenile literature. [1. Washington (D.C.)] I. Title: Washington, DC. II. Title. III. Series.
  F194.3.R53 2003
  975.3–dc21
                                                2003003899

Do you know where you
can find the White House?

It is in Washington, D.C. Washington, D.C., is our nation's capital.

Can you find Washington, D.C., on this map?

It is located between Maryland and Virginia.

George Washington

Washington, D.C., is named for George Washington. He was the first president of the United States.

The letters "D.C." stand for "District of Columbia." The name honors the explorer, Christopher Columbus.

Washington, D.C., has four sections. They are the northwest, southwest, northeast, and southeast.

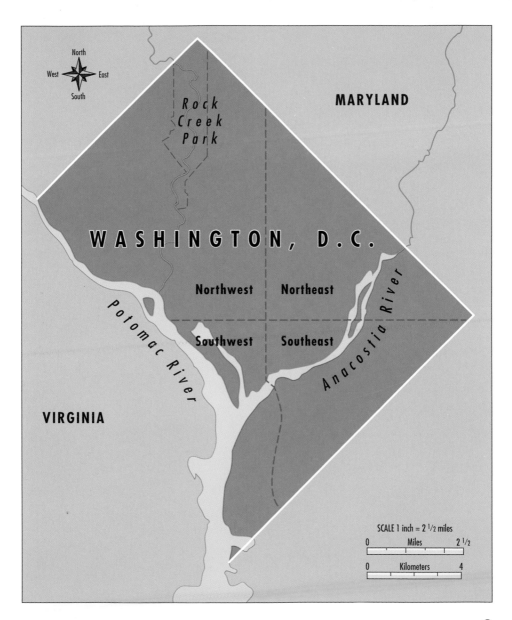

North
West · East
South

Rock
Creek
Park

MARYLAND

WASHINGTON, D.C.

Northwest | Northeast

Southwest | Southeast

Potomac River

Anacostia River

VIRGINIA

SCALE 1 inch = 2 ½ miles

0   Miles   2 ½

0   Kilometers   4

9

10

Rock Creek runs through the city from north to south. Rock Creek Park is a pretty park to visit.

Many people in Washington, D.C., work for the government.

A popular place to visit is the White House. This is where the president lives. It is located in the northwest part of the city.

Most government buildings are located in the northwest.

15

Inside the Capitol building

16

The capitol is where
Congress works.
Congress makes laws.

The Library of Congress
is near the Capitol. It is
the world's largest library.

In 1829, a British scientist named James Smithson gave a lot of money to the American government.

The Smithsonian Institution was started with that money. It has 14 museums (myoo-ZEE-uhms) and one zoo.

National Air and Space Museum

Nine museums are along the Mall. The Mall is a long, grassy park with buildings on all sides.

One of the museums is the National Air and Space Museum. You can see the first airplane there.

The Washington Monument is at one end of the Mall. Visitors can go to the top in an elevator.

Washington, D.C., has trees
and wildlife, too. The district
bird is the wood thrush.

Some streets are lined with cherry trees. The trees were a gift from Japan to the United States.

There are many things to do for fun. Some people like going to the art museum to draw.

Other people enjoy
watching the Washington
Redskins play football.

Washington, D.C., is a great place to visit!

Many people come to the nation's capital because there is so much to do.

Words You Know

cherry blossoms

George Washington

National Air and Space Museum

Rock Creek Park

Washington Monument

White House

wood thrush

31

Index

About the Author

Simone T. Ribke grew up on a horse farm in Maryland and now lives in New York City. She has a degree in education and writes children's books. Simone loves playing football and spending time with her cat.

Photo Credits

Photographs © 2003: Aurora & Quanta Productions/Jose Azel: 20, 30 bottom; Dembinsky Photo Assoc./Greg Gawlowski: 22, 31 top right; Folio, Inc.: 10, 31 top left (Ed Castle), 12 (Rob Crandall), 15 (Pete Souza); Photo Researchers, NY: 24, 31 bottom right (Ron Austing), 19 (Rafael Macia), 16 (Fred Maroon); Photri Inc.: 3, 31 bottom left (Henryk T. Kaiser), 29 (B. Kulik), 25, 30 top left (Richard T. Nowitz); Stockphoto.com/Dennis Brack: 26; Stone/Getty Images/Doug Armand: cover; Superstock, Inc.: 6, 30 top right; Woodfin Camp & Associates/Catherine Karnow: 27.